T0021147

SEWING THE RAINBOW

The Story of Gilbert Baker and the Rainbow Flag

by
GAYLE E. PITMAN, PhD

illustrated by
HOLLY CLIFTON-BROWN

Magination Press • Washington, DC • American Psychological Association

To Laurie McBride, for sharing her personal stories about Gilbert with me—*GP*
To Ed & Lily—*HC-B*

Copyright © 2018 by Gayle Pitman. Illustrations copyright © 2018 by Holly Clifton-Brown. All rights reserved. Except as permitted under the United States Copyright Act of 1976, no part of this publication may be reproduced or distributed in any form or by any means, or stored in a database or retrieval system, without the prior written permission of the publisher.

Published by MAGINATION PRESS®
American Psychological Association
750 First Street NE
Washington, DC 20002

Magination Press is a registered trademark of the American Psychological Association.
For more information about our books, including a complete catalog, please write to us, call 1-800-374-2721, or visit our website at www.apa.org/pubs/magination.

Book design by Gwen Grafft
Printed by Lake Book Manufacturing Inc., Melrose Park, IL

Library of Congress Cataloging-in-Publication Data
Names: Pitman, Gayle E., author. | Clifton-Brown, Holly, illustrator.
Title: Sewing the rainbow: the story of Gilbert Baker and the rainbow flag / by Gayle E. Pitman ; illustrated by Holly Clifton-Brown.
Description: Washington, DC : Magination Press, [2018] | Audience: Age: 4-8.
Identifiers: LCCN 2017046502| ISBN 9781433829024 (hardcover) | ISBN 1433829029 (hardcover)
Subjects: LCSH: Baker, Gilbert, 1951-2017. | Gay activists—United States—Biography—
   Juvenile literature. |Gay liberation movement—United States— Juvenile literature.
Classification: LCC HQ75.8.B345 P58 2018 | DDC 306.76/60973—dc23 LC record
available at https://lccn.loc.gov/2017046502

Manufactured in the United States of America
10 9 8 7 6 5 4 3 2

In a small town in Kansas, where everything
was gray and dull and flat, there was a little boy
who was full of color and sparkle and glitter.
His name was Gilbert.

Gilbert loved visiting his grandmother's clothing store. He'd sit next to her while she sewed and draw beautiful gowns and costumes. Gilbert dreamed of someday bringing these drawings to life.

But one day, his father took away his art supplies
and tore up his drawings.

Surrounded by building blocks and Erector sets, sports gear and slingshots, Gilbert's colorful, sparkly, glittery personality started to fade, and he, too, became gray and dull and flat, just like the Kansas landscape.

"When I grow up," he dreamed,
"I'll go somewhere that's filled with color."

But that didn't happen. Instead, when Gilbert turned eighteen, he received a letter that knocked every last bit of sparkle out of him.

Gilbert hated his dull, flat uniform. And he refused to shoot the gun they gave him. "I won't do it," he said. "I'm not going to carry a gun." They made him do push-ups. They called him ugly names. But Gilbert wouldn't budge. The idea of shooting a gun made him feel sick.

So they sent him to
San Francisco, where
he would never have
to pick up a gun again.

The day Gilbert arrived in San Francisco, he saw MAGIC. Instead of the gray, dull, flat landscape of Kansas, there were rolling green hills, the shimmering blue bay, and a cool white fog wafting over the Golden Gate Bridge. Gilbert was home. Finally, he could breathe. He could be his colorful, sparkly, glittery self.

He thought about his grandmother's clothing store.
He thought about the drawings his father tore up.
And he realized he wanted all of that back.

So Gilbert taught himself to sew, and he created fabulous costumes, just like the ones he drew when he was a little boy.

Word got around fast.

He sewed regalia for
Mama José and her
Imperial Court.

He sewed costumes
for famous singers
like Sylvester.

He sewed banners for protests, marches, and rallies.
Gilbert's creations were everywhere.
He was making the city more and more colorful by the day.

There was just one thing that continued to
blemish their beautiful city. It was a symbol that,
in Gilbert's community, was a constant reminder of evil.

"We need a new logo," his friend
Harvey said to him one day.
And Gilbert got an idea.

He bought huge bolts of cotton fabric, buckets of dye, and a LOT of thread. Then he gathered up all his friends and got to work.

They cut the fabric into long strips, dyed them in big trash cans, then headed to the local laundromat to rinse and dry the strips. They ironed the creases so the fabric was nice and smooth.

Then, Gilbert began to sew.

They worked until dawn.

By the time the sun rose, Gilbert and his friends had
created two beautiful rainbow flags. But their work
wasn't over. "A flag belongs in the wind," Gilbert said.

The big day arrived. A crowd gathered around City Hall.
Gilbert held his breath. Would people understand his flags?

Up they went! The flags unfurled,
flooding the sky with a spectrum
of colors. The city radiated with color
and sparkle and glitter.

And the crowd lit up,
like gold at the end of the rainbow.

Today, the rainbow flag is everywhere. Even in the small town in Kansas where Gilbert grew up.

Wherever you see a rainbow flag, you'll know that it's okay to be your colorful, sparkly, glittery self.

Reader Note

Imagine what it might have been like to grow up in the 1950s. World War II had ended, soldiers were coming back home, and the "Rosie the Riveter" era had come to an abrupt halt. The era ushered in the "Golden Age of Television," featuring shows like *I Love Lucy*, *Ozzie and Harriet*, *Father Knows Best*, *The Donna Reed Show*, and *Leave It to Beaver*. All of these shows promoted traditional White middle-class heterosexual nuclear families, where men dressed in suits and took on the role of family provider, and women in dresses and aprons spent most of their time in the kitchen. Underneath the happy-go-lucky veneer of these TV shows was a deep, pervasive fear of communists, leftists, radicals, gender nonconformity, and homosexuality. This is what life was like on June 2, 1951, when Gilbert Baker was born.

From the beginning, Gilbert was different. Instead of running around and getting dirty like the other boys, he liked to spend time in his grandmother's clothing store while she sewed. To pass the time, Gilbert drew elaborate costumes, ball gowns, and other fashionable creations.

As Gilbert got older, his father became more and more upset by his gender-nonconforming behaviors. At first, his father took a subtle approach, encouraging Gilbert to play with building blocks and Erector sets. Later, when it was clear that Gilbert wasn't interested in these traditional masculine pursuits, his father tore up his drawings, took away his art supplies, and pushed him harder to act like a "real boy." When Gilbert graduated from high school, he received a draft notice from the Army, and his parents were hopeful that this would "man him up." It didn't; Gilbert refused to shoot his military-issued M16, and eventually he was given an honorable discharge and sent to San Francisco to work as a medic.

When Gilbert arrived in San Francisco in 1972, he felt hopeful for the first time. He'd been suffering from depression for a long time, having attempted suicide shortly after his honorable discharge. However, San Francisco introduced him to David Bowie and the glam rock scene, and Gilbert saw a place for himself in that subculture. "The community saved my life," Gilbert said in an interview. Shortly after moving to the city, Gilbert befriended a woman who owned a Singer sewing machine, and he taught himself to sew. "I wanted to dress like David Bowie, but I didn't have any money," he said in an interview. Later, Gilbert bought his own sewing machine, and he began sewing costumes for himself. Word got around quickly about Gilbert's talents; when he joined the Sisters of Perpetual Indulgence, other Sisters asked him to sew habits and wimples decked out in sequins, feathers, and rhinestones. He sewed costumes for drag performers like Sylvester. He designed and sewed regalia for José Sarria's Imperial Court. Moreover, gay men were moving to the city and flocking to the Castro district, leading to the creation of one of the most famous gay neighborhoods in the world. And he created banners for various protests, marches, and rallies. Eventually, Gilbert became a vexillographer (a flag maker), which became his best-known form of activism.

As the gay liberation movement gained traction, by the mid-1970s the gay community was much more vocal and visible than ever before. Gilbert had sewn countless banners, and at the time, the pink triangle was the only real "symbol" used to designate the gay community. Gilbert found this particular image, a constant reminder of the persecution of gay people during the Holocaust, to be quite depressing. His friend Harvey Milk agreed with him. "We need a new logo," Harvey once said—and Gilbert decided to take on the challenge.

Why the rainbow? Gilbert was asked this question many times throughout his life. He usually answered by saying, "Rainbows are from nature," reminding us that it's natural to be whomever we are, and to love whomever we love. He also noted throughout his life that, as a symbol, the rainbow exists in every culture, showing how we're all connected. And the rainbow is mentioned in the Bible: Genesis 9:13 states, "I have set my rainbow in the clouds, and it will be the sign of the covenant between me and the earth." This verse resonated with Gilbert, and he found it ironic that conservative, anti-LGBTQ Christians routinely engaged in efforts to "reclaim the rainbow," so to speak.

And why a flag? Gilbert always knew the power of flags; he was once quoted as saying, "A flag is torn from the soul of the people." But it was probably the bicentennial celebration in 1976 that inspired Gilbert to create his own iconic flag. That year, American flags were everywhere, from Jasper Johns paintings to designer T-shirts—and for the first time, Gilbert really understood the power of the flag. If he could design a symbol to be used on a flag, that symbol would become instantly recognizable, and that would give the LGBTQ community more power and visibility than ever before.

The first two flags were a labor of love from the community, and it took a group of about 30 people to create them. Most of his friends had no idea how to sew, but they could do other things to help. Cleve Jones, one of Gilbert's best friends, helped raise money to purchase supplies to create the flags.

Other friends helped cut and iron the fabric. Gilbert's friend Fairy Argyle Rainbow taught everyone how to dye the fabric using natural dyes. They dyed the fabric at the Gay Community Center, located at the time at 330 Grove Street. Then they snuck into the laundromat late at night so they could rinse the dye out—despite the fact that there were signs that said "DO NOT DYE." (In an interview, Gilbert joked that they washed out the machines with Clorox and hoped that the people who did their wash in the morning didn't end up with pink underwear!) Back at the Gay Community Center, the group dried, ironed, and, with the help of Gilbert's friend James McNamara, sewed the strips together. They worked all night long, and by dawn, the flags were completed.

On June 25, 1978, the day of the San Francisco Gay Freedom Day Parade, the flags were raised for the first time in the United Nations Plaza. The original flags had eight stripes—pink, red, orange, yellow, green, turquoise, blue, and violet. One of the two flags had tie-dyed stars made by Fairy Argyle Rainbow. That year, the Gay Freedom Day celebration had special meaning to the community—Harvey Milk had just been elected to the Board of Supervisors, and this was his first parade in that role, as well as his first opportunity to see the community's new "logo" unveiled. Sadly, this was also his last Gay Freedom Day parade; he and Mayor George Moscone were assassinated by Dan White on November 27, 1978.

Gilbert hand-sewed a number of rainbow flags after the initial unveiling, and the rainbow flag as a symbol for the LGBTQ community caught on quickly. Soon, the demand for them was so great that Gilbert couldn't keep up with the work, and the Paramount Flag Company took over and began to make the flags commercially. At the time, pink dye and turquoise dye were difficult to come by,

designate the gay community. Gilbert found this particular image, a constant reminder of the persecution of gay people during the Holocaust, to be quite depressing. His friend Harvey Milk agreed with him. "We need a new logo," Harvey once said—and Gilbert decided to take on the challenge.

Why the rainbow? Gilbert was asked this question many times throughout his life. He usually answered by saying, "Rainbows are from nature," reminding us that it's natural to be whomever we are, and to love whomever we love. He also noted throughout his life that, as a symbol, the rainbow exists in every culture, showing how we're all connected. And the rainbow is mentioned in the Bible: Genesis 9:13 states, "I have set my rainbow in the clouds, and it will be the sign of the covenant between me and the earth." This verse resonated with Gilbert, and he found it ironic that conservative, anti-LGBTQ Christians routinely engaged in efforts to "reclaim the rainbow," so to speak.

And why a flag? Gilbert always knew the power of flags; he was once quoted as saying, "A flag is torn from the soul of the people." But it was probably the bicentennial celebration in 1976 that inspired Gilbert to create his own iconic flag. That year, American flags were everywhere, from Jasper Johns paintings to designer T-shirts—and for the first time, Gilbert really understood the power of the flag. If he could design a symbol to be used on a flag, that symbol would become instantly recognizable, and that would give the LGBTQ community more power and visibility than ever before.

The first two flags were a labor of love from the community, and it took a group of about 30 people to create them. Most of his friends had no idea how to sew, but they could do other things to help. Cleve Jones, one of Gilbert's best friends, helped raise money to purchase supplies to create the flags.

Other friends helped cut and iron the fabric. Gilbert's friend Fairy Argyle Rainbow taught everyone how to dye the fabric using natural dyes. They dyed the fabric at the Gay Community Center, located at the time at 330 Grove Street. Then they snuck into the laundromat late at night so they could rinse the dye out—despite the fact that there were signs that said "DO NOT DYE." (In an interview, Gilbert joked that they washed out the machines with Clorox and hoped that the people who did their wash in the morning didn't end up with pink underwear!) Back at the Gay Community Center, the group dried, ironed, and, with the help of Gilbert's friend James McNamara, sewed the strips together. They worked all night long, and by dawn, the flags were completed.

On June 25, 1978, the day of the San Francisco Gay Freedom Day Parade, the flags were raised for the first time in the United Nations Plaza. The original flags had eight stripes—pink, red, orange, yellow, green, turquoise, blue, and violet. One of the two flags had tie-dyed stars made by Fairy Argyle Rainbow. That year, the Gay Freedom Day celebration had special meaning to the community—Harvey Milk had just been elected to the Board of Supervisors, and this was his first parade in that role, as well as his first opportunity to see the community's new "logo" unveiled. Sadly, this was also his last Gay Freedom Day parade; he and Mayor George Moscone were assassinated by Dan White on November 27, 1978.

Gilbert hand-sewed a number of rainbow flags after the initial unveiling, and the rainbow flag as a symbol for the LGBTQ community caught on quickly. Soon, the demand for them was so great that Gilbert couldn't keep up with the work, and the Paramount Flag Company took over and began to make the flags commercially. At the time, pink dye and turquoise dye were difficult to come by, so those two stripes were eliminated when the flags went into commercial production. The iconic flag became what we know it to be today—red, orange, yellow, green, blue, and purple stripes.

Gilbert continued to sew flags, banners, costumes, and dresses for many years. In 1994, he sewed a mile-long rainbow flag to commemorate the 25th anniversary of the Stonewall riots. Fifteen years later, in 2009, Gilbert honored the 40th anniversary of Stonewall by sewing a ruby-sequined banner—partly to recognize that "ruby" anniversary, and partly as a symbolic nod to the film that mirrored his own life in so many ways, *The Wizard of Oz*.

Gilbert Baker died in his sleep on March 31, 2017.

About the Author

Gayle E. Pitman, PhD, is a professor of psychology and women's studies at Sacramento City College. Her teaching and writing focuses on gender and sexual orientation, and she has worked extensively with the lesbian, gay, bisexual, transgender, and queer (LGBTQ) community. She is the author of *This Day In June*, which won the 2015 Stonewall Book Award—Mike Morgan and Larry Romans Children's and Young Adult Literature Award. She is also the author of *When You Look Out the Window*, a picture book biography of lesbian couple Phyllis Lyon and Del Martin, and *Feminism From A to Z*, a book for teens of all genders.

About the Illustrator

Holly Clifton-Brown is an illustrator and artist based in Somerset, England. She graduated from the University of the West of England (UWE Bristol) in 2008, and has since published several picture books and illustrations for an array of international publishing companies and clients. Her work combines traditional painting, mixed media, and collage with contemporary techniques to create a unique and imaginative visual language. When Holly is not drawing, you'll find her in the bath tub, out walking in the countryside with her family, fermenting vegetables, and having micro adventures with her son Ossian and dog Olive.

About Magination Press

Magination Press is an imprint of the American Psychological Association, the largest scientific and professional organization representing psychologists in the United States and the largest association of psychologists worldwide.